# of sword and

spindle

Amandine Castonguay

BookLeaf
Publishing

India | USA | UK

Presentation by *BookLeaf Publishing*

Web: www.bookleafpub.com

E-mail: info@bookleafpub.com

ISBN: 978-93-5744-400-2

First edition 2022

DEDICATION

For the Eros to my Psyche, may we always dance together in the milk light of moon.

# of sword and spindle

The soft opal edges
of your stolen thievens kiss
And my forgotten marble daydreams
both leave my bones in bliss

I thought I saw you watching
from the waning crescent moon,
I almost swore I heard you weeping,
singing a broken harpist's tune

There is a tree in which I'm buried
down far deep beneath the roots,
There is a lighthouse that you dream of
in which brews a storm in you

Maybe somewhere you are waiting
in a spiny ochre wood,
Perhaps the king was lying
or I misunderstood

You are the dark in that I flourish,
You are the light between the pines,
There's a clearing in the forest
where we shall stand the test of time

A tiny serpents tail
through my viney weathered heart,
A mirage I can't compete with,
I suppose true love is a lost art

You're a bridge I haven't built yet
so there's nothing here to burn,
An ultra violence I can't pinpoint
although it comes in many forms

A secret solace slayer,
your sword has torn me all to shreds

So please keep all your needles,
my spindle is running out of thread

a tiger in my reading room

There is a tiger in my reading room
Beside oil paintings
velvet chairs
I cling like a moth
to the light that he brings
In this circus maximus
we're a heavenly pair

You say that I'm tragic
completely divine
You are my eternal Valentine
But blue buttons
fall in the winter
And cold days
turn me to ice

So you relit the hearth
to warm up my
bones
Medusa could never turn me to stone
And your eyes
hold a fire like Odin
While your fangs
they rarely come out

But,

I know there's a
shark in your river
And sometimes that
clouds me with
doubt

I used to be scared to go for a dip
But now I dive in,

Just hoping
he doesn't
come out

le chevalier aux fleurs

In the roseate glade of a whispering wood
efflorescence reflects across echoing ore
An opaque blacksmith once forged
for a gent far less reclaimed
But now on the knight's body
this armor does brace

In gleaming daydreams,
sweet blooms flourish in spring
Amongst verdant silk leaves,
botanic suitors and thieves

As they horde 'round the horseman
with adamantine complexion
Luring voices of sayters
fill his affection

Then they all cloak around him
porcelain skin bare to the bone
Their vines spine their way up
over marrow and stone

Beside the glistening light
he succumbs to their pleas
Then flower maidens devour him

their endless love a disease

Now if you go there to find him
in the posy filled wood
You will see rusted old armor
where a brave knight once stood

cobweb-like heart

There's angels in the architecture
Eros is searching the missed connections
you told me not to paint it blue
ambivalence, crescendos too

my lion on his regal post
he warns me that I'm just a ghost
"diaphanous, cobweb-like heart,
you are noble, play the part"

But I am always too demure
evanescent, are his words
They hold me like the setting sun
but I am always on the run

from labyrinthine
hearts and wine

to penumbra times
sweet love,
divine

to my lover at his humble post
to mossy leaves and spindly oaks
to rivers and riparian trees

to the elixir of the earth and seas

for I am strong without sharp teeth
I don't need a lion belittling me

the church at auver

Opalescent white across cerulean skies
Ochre fields draped in vivid sunflowers
A lonely midnight shoe hanging from its bower

A thought-provoking face I asked to paint her
then to a crimson barn I take my shelter
Azure drops of water begin leaking through
but I study my cream brushstrokes as I think of
you

Theo, I coddle the green faerie
she's seeped in every muscle
I think my mind was lost
somewhere back in Brussels
But don't you see I'm where I need to be
I think when I'm gone they'll come to visit me

Gauguin left sometime back in December
a lonely slate Christmas I won't remember
Sometimes I think they don't understand the
blues
It's hard to say I saw gold hues in you

From an ash window my soul is free

I paint the town below, let it embody me
There is no beautiful way to say I'm alone
but this night sky somewhat feels like home

It's late July now,
the raven crows are out
The olive trees bloom
near the wheat fields of doubt
Perhaps I will go and paint today
maybe this one will finally earn me praise

gingerbread dreams

gingerbread dreams
laying out in the dawn
turning clouds into camelot
with sheer vision and song

you write to me, poems
these words like church pews
cradle me safely
as if i'm god's only muse

so love sick like a cherub
with a quiver of hearts
all forged out of silver
and burning with darts

so safe like a painting
on a museum wall
guarded by sentries
never to fall

gingerbread dreams
planting flowers in spring
turning dirt into warlocks
made of cabbage and kings

letters from hyacinthus

Do not weep at my gravestone, Apollo
don't whisper my name in debt to the moon

Do not never forget me, Apollo
I pray for my ghost to leave your side soon

Do not water my flowers, Apollo
they shall wither to earth like my body has done

Do not think of me often, Apollo
I am so far away and death can't be undone

Do not make timeworn skies dark, Apollo
there is wheat to be sown beside wars to be won

Do not stay by my deathbed, Apollo
do not weave my name through the setting sun

king of hearts

I am a grandiose cathedral
I am an old opera song
I am a chapel in pieces
yet here you are

I love like a religion
drink through cinnamon straws
I've always forgiven
while I'm changing the locks

If you enter my bethel
and don't burn it down
You'll be the first to be faith-ful
so I give you the crown

The king of my heart
in this house made of cards
The bringer of hope
to the funeral parlor

The lion is jaded
so I put him away
I opened the windows
I dusted the panes

I am a grandiose cathedral
that you've entered to pray
The first time I've opened my doors
and not turned them away

sleepy hollow

An eternal town of autumn
orange hues cast over the hills
It's darkness calls upon them
glowing reds cascade down from his quill

A headless apparition,
hanging in the forest like a coat
It waits all summer long
for September's chill to help it float

A scarecrow doppelgänger,
with a face so strange and rare,
He often thinks he hears things in the woods
that are not there

The paintings hanging languidly
sculptures in the trees
When the twilight comes for you
you will feel it in the breeze

But what about the lady fair,
who haunts you like a ghost
Who will guide her down the trail,
if the cold air becomes your host?

It's out for blood, don't you eye?
It wants the roses red
So go safely in the night time now,
or it will have your head

my dearest, endymion

Nestled in a faraway cave, my love
I kiss the creases from your gentle lace
What ever are you dreaming in that lovesome
head of yours,
could you be wondering if the moon has a fair
face?

I read to you, sweet poetry
beneath the dripping of the crest
I hear the thrumming of your heart
when I lay my face down upon your breast

I come to you, every night
my skin glowing in the shadows
Your painted face,
your iron grace,
I would follow through the hallows

Sometimes I yearn to hear your voice
gaze into sparkling eyes
But consciousness is best well kept
for another time

My lover of a hundred years
I'd sail a thousand ships

Just to reach your sleeping form
Just to kiss your heart shaped lips

Nothing could keep me
from this cave, my love
Nothing could take me from your side
Nothing could tear me
from this grave, my love

Not the gods
Not the gallows
Not the brine

the briny deep

The briny deep is calling me
her waters sing ancient soliloquies
This tempest of gold,
her grasp on my throat
I sense that I'm being
pulled down below

Beneath the sallow sunset
Beneath the white capped seas
Where I can lay to rest
amongst Neptunian trees

Like an empyrean star
my soul takes to the sky
I leave my body back where
other expired men lie

"An eternal resting spot",
she speaks of sweet death
Like it's a pleasant embrace
Like she's Lady Macbeth

So I go there to her
I let her sink me deep down
The sea is always more loving

of those eager to drown

antique ill-fated lovers

Gossamer threads
spinning webs overhead
The marriage of strings
sewn into butterfly wings

Antique ill-fated lovers
painted on paper dolls
Telling tales of the past
heading Psyche's call

The dire fate of Ophelia
The lovely Lady Shallot
Ineffable trials
of heartbreak and woe

Mondegreen listening
a twist of the words
Murmurous meddling
a pastiche artist's slurs

The river bank rising
The sun sinking low
When the night
turns the lights out
I close my book

and go home

eros' fountain

The words bleeding from the rafters
How they haunt like a siren's song
How they crawl through your ears,
and wreck you with tears
How they echo off stones,
like heartbreak in your bones

But don't you hear Eros' fountain?
How the water calls like a ghost
How the woes of past lovers
fall with the stream
How this pulls at your heart strings,
upmost

I tried to warn my dear knight
that those woods had been ridden of light
But he went anyway,
the vines dragged him astray
And his voice still plagues me,
his plight

The words dousing the woodland
The ochre is all turning blue
You'd rather touch death,
than caress my skin

But mountains,
I would climb
for you

the holy grail

Behind the sullen face of
the milk light of moon
Beneath the charred bones
inside hades tomb
The secrets I keep will never be spoken
I hold them inside me
my heart's cellar door is always open

Behind herbal rosaries
hollowed oak trees
Through the hagged stone's hole
Through the voice in the breeze

I hold it close to my chest
like an armored out vest
This secret will save me from
arrows and quest

Under mossy old stones
Under scarabs and bone
In the midnight hag's eye
here the answers do lie

Above smog clouds overhead
In the cells Remus bled

Under miles of snow
In the place no one will go

magic in burning

The heat waves waft up like
smoke in the sunlight
Everything is magic
when you look at it
just right

The wildflowers are dead
so I've been painting them hues
I've been staring too long at
silver linings and dew

As the house burns down
there's such a violent beauty
In watching curtains fall
dreamlike soft melancholy

I remember standing on the road,
I was six years old
The warmth from the fire
biting at the cold

I recall thinking then,
that there's so much unexplained
Why do I find magic in burning
and see lights in the rain

There is vast beauty in death
There is sweet sugar in pain
There are halcyon times in death
but love and life,
just the same

lovelorn pirate

I woke up on a mountain peak
between the cogon grass and dew
I sat up rather slowly
as abandoned lovers do

But do you hear me weeping,
just like a fountain thrum?
Do you see my shadow fading,
as my blood turns into rum?

The River wouldn't take me yet,
it said not my time has come
The bears and badgers ignore my form,
they say I'm not quite wild plum

I remember when you found me
all freckled face and fear
You turned me into a menace
not even brave men would leer

So, what happened to grave robbings and golden
nights spent on the pier?
What happened to all those pillage tales you'd
whisper in my ear?

Are white capped seas and bleak sunsets more
alluring than my kiss?
If you have your faithful brutes and the king's
loot, am I not something that you miss?

Oh, pirate lord, how I wish to be back,
upon your lawless barge
Amongst guttersnipes and manly gripes,
instead of perched upon this log

Meadow and dirt can not compare
to mildewed oak and yew
Tranquility is a fair fate
but my lord, it can't outdo

words of honey

Sweet moonlight sheen upon your face,
paying out crimes with prayers and lace
Those cloudy silken words of blue
my eyelids shut and I see you

Anguish Poe disease, a twist of fate
which led me through the sinners gates
Soft lonely me drank yellow paint
then pondered why my chest still ached

Their words of honey rot my teeth
through trying times and solemn peace
Through evergreens and golden suns,
I finally became someone

The strength of seven swords acquired,
I took my grime and made it wild
I sewed back all my faulty seems
I drudged out all the good in me

For I was lost a long long time
between the brush and columbine
Behind the madness and the haze
I sat waiting there for better days

The woodland sounds forevermore,
those sunrise eyes that I adore

And in the night I walked alone,
but felt like I was coming home

the shadow of a mulberry tree

The solvent drains
from the somber veil above
no cobalt sky today
no more setting sun

The brick walled city
doesn't feel the same
And it's forbidden love and a dagger
that are to blame

And if you go down to
the town that Semiramis built
The lonely chink in the wall
has no more whispers spilt

The fires of the night burn out
The sunshine betrays the frost
Under the shadow of a Mulberry tree
I sense what innocence has lost

And when the weeping moon
floods the dark forest bed
I can see the ancient tree's fruit
change from white to red

Right beside Ninus' tomb
their souls swim in a cool spring
They were paramours
them and their love slain before rings

Only the gods and the night
witnessed their treacherous flights
And their apostles still cry
under an azurite sky

Beneath a spindling tree
our martyrs went to die
And doused across a forest floor
their love still lies

heavenly sword

This clandestine castle of books
dead butterflies, soft looks
Silken hearts tied on strings
paper flowers, chryselephantine

I entered here in the blinding dark
I didn't see a light but I felt the spark

Flowers grew from our blood
like a hyacinth
As you lead me out
of this labyrinth

Now there's a rose gold dove
on the window pane
There's a roof over my head
when it rains
There's a pulling on a
harpist's strings
There's a card I read of
the pentacle king

Through these creeping vines
I found a crystal well,
just before my apparition

could cast her spell

Then in the golden hour
I returned to me,
like the moon calling out
to an ancient sea

It was, me in my house of cards
around fields of inflorescence

And you, with your heavenly sword

Now I'm dancing
under an apple tree
You're the sun
shining down on me
You're the distant howl
on the first full moon
You're the feeling
I sense is
coming soon

the funeral

You once towered the land
like a roman statue on guard
The closest thing
to permanence besides rock
Something that humans
can't touch

How you nourished the grove
with your shelter and shade
All the ardor you gave
until they carved out
your grave

See, try to understand
that humans have an odd way
of ruining good things
of shortening their stay
in the treasures of earth
in the greed of good kings
in the temperance of love
in the heart of wild beings

So they brought in a black coal train
So they brought in a hearse
and they stripped you down bare

and they felt no remorse

All those years now behind you
like they never were there
Will the bluebirds remember?
Will the howling foxes care?

Now I stand here before you
nearly praying on sight
Like I'm attending a funeral
for a great pine dressed in lights

museo cerralbo

Museo Cerralbo
Poems in your petticoat
Take me to a museum
Sketch me next to Gauguin

Take me to the wheat fields
Where my first love went to die
Hold me in the flowing grass
Like you're the only one for I

I'd never been in love back then
Except with art and intoxicants
But that was such a labyrinth
it broke my heart
it robbed my sense

Museo Cerralbo
Won't you be my Camelot?
In this dulcet decadence,
won't you be my cherished thought?

I hold you like a talisman,
a paper weight
a steady hand

You can hold me like a talisman,
your lighthouse
your guarded land
Museo Cerralbo